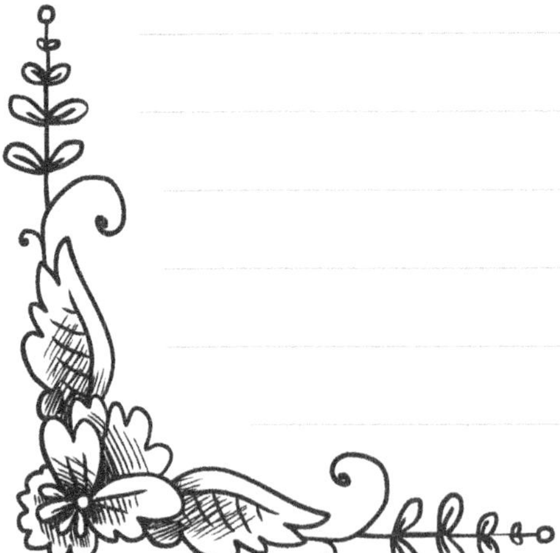

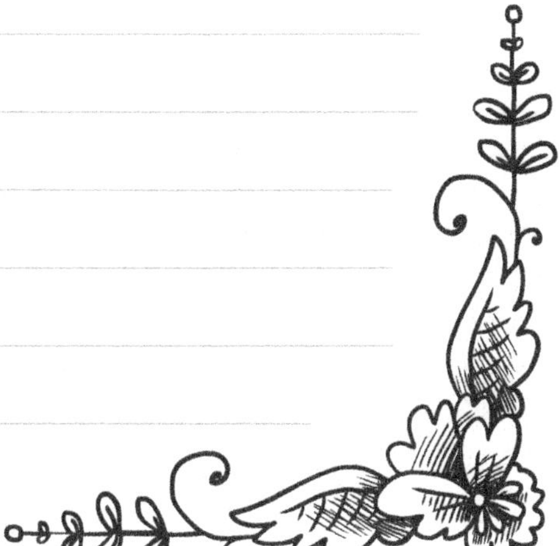

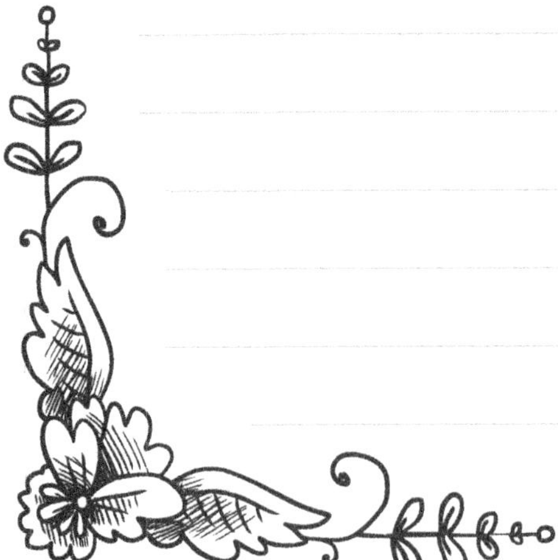

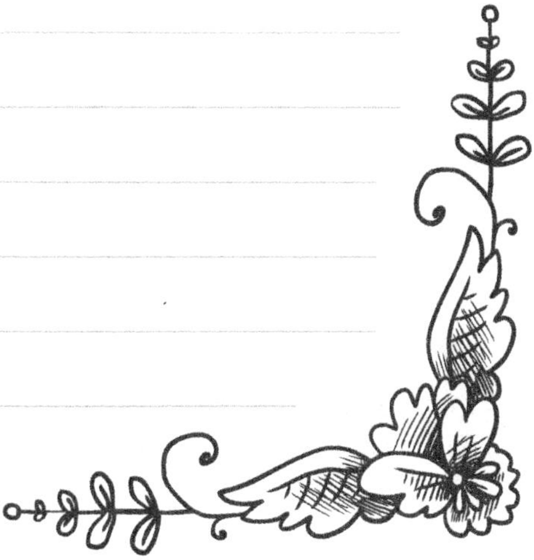

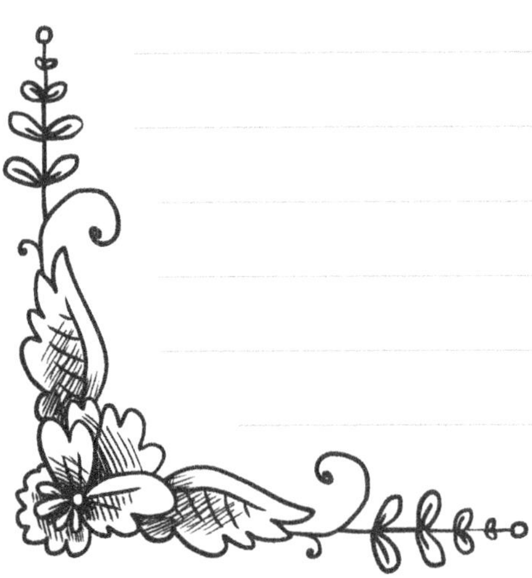

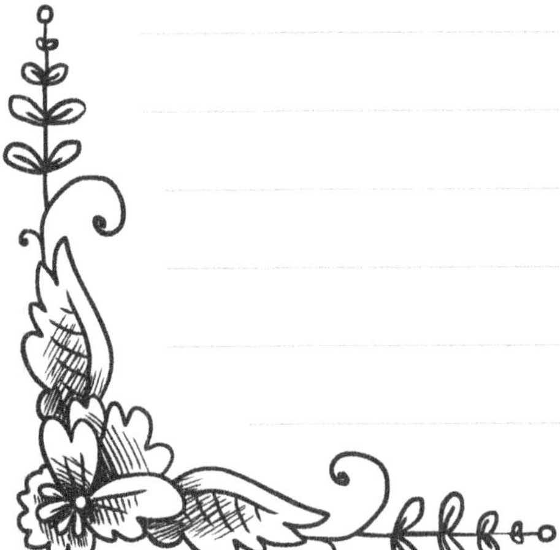

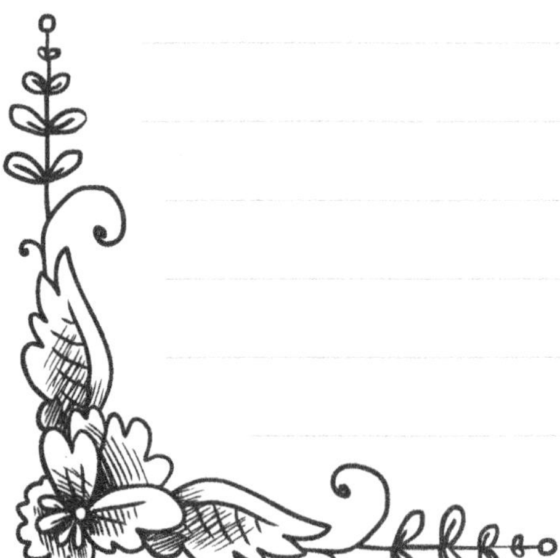

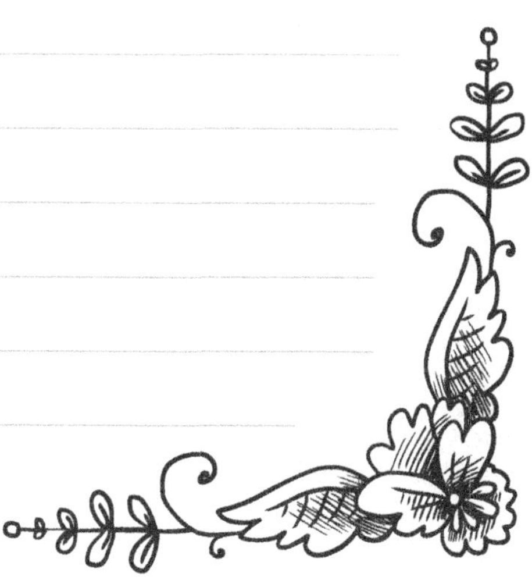

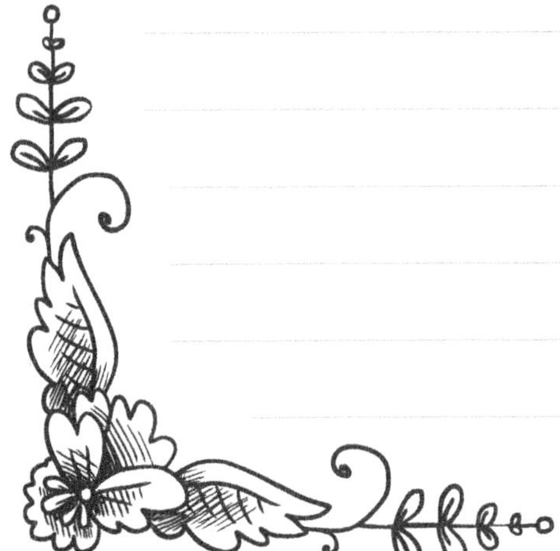

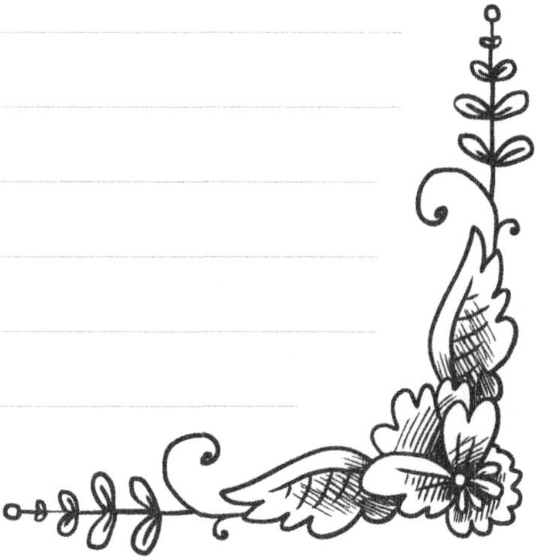

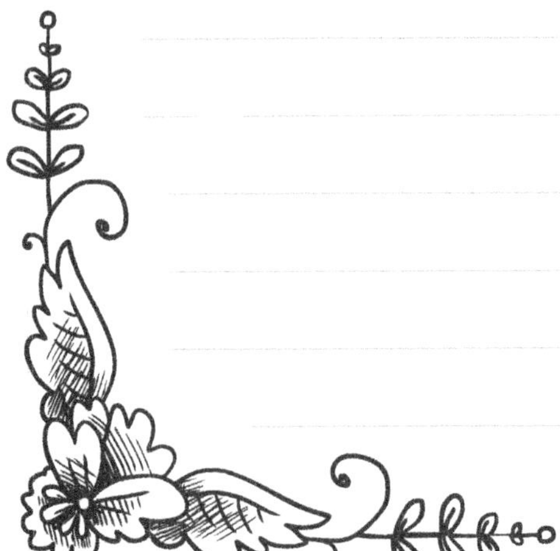

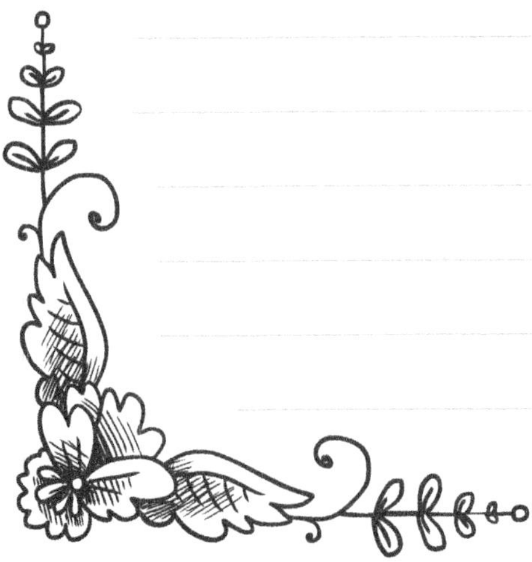

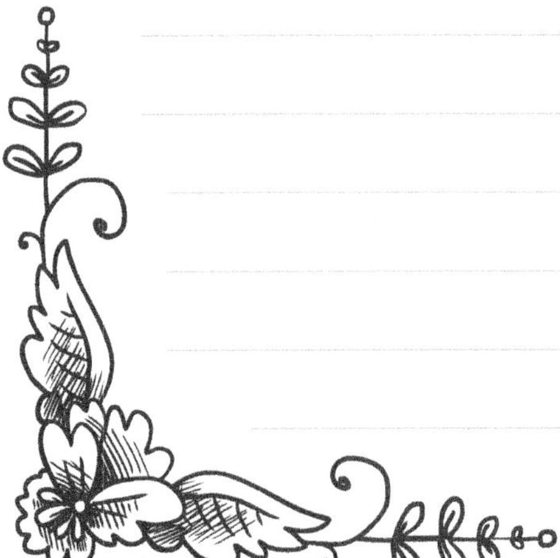

Made in the USA
Monee, IL
04 August 2021

74942397R00073